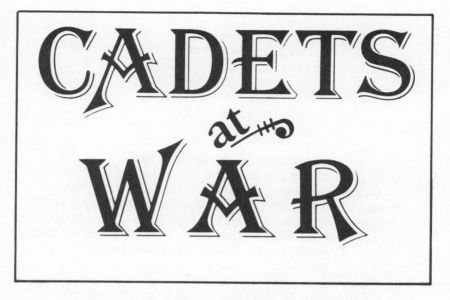

CADETS at WAR

The True Story of Teenage Heroism
at the Battle of New Market

Susan Provost Beller

SHOE TREE PRESS
WHITE HALL, VIRGINIA

Published by Shoe Tree Press, an imprint of
Betterway Publications, Inc.
P.O. Box 219
Crozet, VA 22932
(804) 823-5661

Cover design by Rick Britton
Cover painting, "Charge of the New Market Cadets," by
Benjamin West Clinedinst, VMI Class of 1880.
Photograph of cover painting courtesy of Michael Latil
Photographs courtesy of Virginia Military Institute
Archives, Virginia Military Institute, and W. Michael Beller
Typography by Park Lane Associates

Cataloging-in-Publication Data

Beller, Susan Provost
    Cadets at war : the true story of teenage heroism at the Battle of
New Market / Susan Provost Beller.
      p. cm.
    Includes bibliographical references and index.
    Summary: Discusses the role of the Virginia Military Institute
cadets in the Battle of New Market in 1864.
    ISBN 1-55870-196-6 (hardcover) : $9.95
    1. New Market, Battle of, 1864--Juvenile literature. 2. Virginia
Military Institute--History--19th century--Juvenile literature.
[1. New Market, Battle of, 1864. 2. United States--History--Civil
War, 1861-1865--Campaigns. 3. Virginia Military Institute-
-History--19th century.] I. Title.
E476.64.B44 1991
973.7'36--dc20
                       90-21952
                             CIP
                             AC

Printed in the United States of America
0 9 8 7 6 5 4 3 2 1

To My Father
Edward Roland Provost
July 23, 1926 — March 24, 1989
who gave Me
Vermont
and the dreams I live by

ACKNOWLEDGMENTS

It would be impossible to thank enough all of the people affiliated with the Virginia Military Institute for all their assistance in hunting down all of the Materials that made this book possible. I was given access to enough information to write a dozen books and the enthusiasm expressed by everyone I met made the researching exciting. First and foremost I would like to thank Diane B. Jacob, who oversees the Archives at Preston Library, VMI, and her assistant, Pat Wohlrab, who gave me a guided tour of the Archives. Their knowledge of the primary source material is phenomenal, and they showed incredible patience as I continually asked for more and more information. Second, my thanks to everyone affiliated with the two museums—the one at VMI and the one at the New Market Battlefield Historical Park. Both are directed by Keith Gibson and he and his staff were always helpful, no matter what the request—from photographing individual items to scheduling appointments with cadets. Working with Frances G. Good, Curator of the New Market Battlefield Historical Park, and with Judy Haviland and Lize Madden at the VMI Museum was always an enjoyable experience. Also at VMI, my thanks to Major Harold Willcockson, Deputy Commandant of Cadets, whose personal interest in my project led him to take time from a very busy day to provide me with a tour of the barracks. Finally, my thanks to Cadet Christopher Whittaker (VMI 1990) and Cadet John D. Shorter (VMI 1991) who graciously consented to be interviewed about the VMI experience.

People who read manuscripts really don't get enough thanks for the job they do. My husband, W. Michael Beller, and my three children, Mike, Jennie, and Sean, read the manuscript at many different stages and were always very forthcoming with comments ("You know, this part doesn't make any sense at all.") and suggestions. As a reader, my thanks go also to Carol Taggart, a teacher at the school where I am librarian, who made the mistake of asking how the project was doing one day and found that people who ask that kind of question end up reading manuscripts.

My thanks also to my editor, Susan Lewis, who was willing to traipse all over Lexington and New Market one day in our search for the right photos for this book.

Last, but never least, my appreciation to my husband, who served not just as a reader but also as photographer for the photos taken at New Market, as chauffeur, and as moral support at the times when it seemed I would never get this book finished.

PREFACE

As a speaker for many years and as author of *Roots for Kids*, I spend a good deal of time talking to school and youth groups. I almost always start with the same story. It only takes two or three minutes to tell but, by the time I have finished it, the kids are usually listening very intently. Every time I tell this story, at least one child (and usually more than one) comes up to me at the end of the talk and asks where they can find out more. Sadly, I am forced to tell them that nothing has been written for kids about this event. Many times I have been asked to write this "story."

What story is this that captures student interest so immediately and holds it so intensely? The story is that of the Virginia Military Institute cadets fighting in the Battle of New Market during the Civil War. More than any other story I have told to groups, this one seems to captivate young listeners and give them a real sense of what it must have felt like to be young and fighting for your cause during the Civil War.

And now, THE STORY . . .

CONTENTS

Chapter 1

SETTING THE SCENE

Imagine for a moment that you are a teenage boy living in the South during the Civil War in the Spring of 1864. You are a student at a military academy in the Shenandoah Valley of Virginia. You may have seen your father, uncles, older brothers, even grandfathers go off to fight to protect the land you love so much. You are impatient to be old enough to join the fight yourself. Instead, you're stuck at the Virginia Military Institute, learning strategy and tactics and practicing drills while everyone around you seems to be involved in the real thing—WAR.

What makes you even more impatient is the fact that you know you are located in one of the most important areas in Virginia in terms of military planning and strategy. The Union troops have been stopped every time they have tried to capture Richmond, the capital of the Confederacy. Since they can't get there directly, they've been trying to sneak around by coming the back way through the Shenandoah Valley. One hundred and twenty miles north of where your school is located in Lexington, Virginia is the town of Winchester, which has changed hands seventy times during the course of this three-year-old war.

As always in the spring, when the armies leave

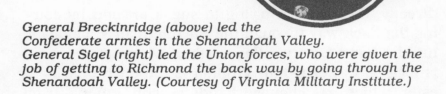

*General Breckinridge (above) led the
Confederate armies in the Shenandoah Valley.
General Sigel (right) led the Union forces, who were given the
job of getting to Richmond the back way by going through the
Shenandoah Valley. (Courtesy of Virginia Military Institute.)*

their winter camps, there is talk of the Union troops trying again to march on Richmond. This spring there is a new general in charge of the Union troops in the Valley. He has been given the difficult job of moving through the Valley to Staunton to keep the Confederate defenders distracted while the main Union army tries to reach Richmond. This new general is Franz Sigel, and he commands an army of 19,000 men. His opponent, commanding the Confederate army in the Valley, is Major General John C. Breckinridge. His job will be to stop Sigel from advancing in the Valley. To do this he has an army of 6,600 men. General Breckinridge needs more men, not only to fight but to serve as reserve troops during the battle to come. The Superintendent of the Virginia Military Institute volunteers to send the Corps of Cadets, made up of about 280 cadets from the school, to join the rest of the Confederate troops. The General decides to accept his offer. For you as a student at VMI, your chance has finally come.

Imagine the excitement you and your fellow cadets feel as you hear the news. Finally, you will be able to take part in this great fight. And of course you know that the cadets will be the bravest of all the men on the battlefield. You are filled with youthful dreams of glory and honor. And all of you are only fifteen to nineteen years old.

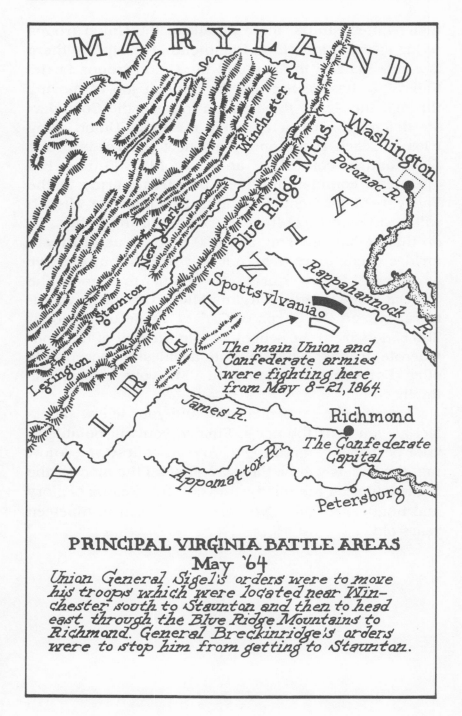

PRINCIPAL VIRGINIA BATTLE AREAS
May '64

Union General Sigel's orders were to move his troops which were located near Winchester south to Staunton and then to head east through the Blue Ridge Mountains to Richmond. General Breckinridge's orders were to stop him from getting to Staunton.

Chapter 2

WAITING

Being a student at the Virginia Military Institute during the Civil War was both good and bad. The good part was knowing that General Lee and the leaders of the Confederacy were counting on you to help train troops for the fighting and to become an officer yourself when you finished your schooling. The bad part was that the wait to get out and fight was so terribly long and you couldn't help worrying that by the time you got old enough, the whole war would be over and you would have missed all the excitement.

Many of the boys attending school at VMI were not strangers to the war going on around them. Many of them had already seen the effects of this long war on their own families. When you read some of the stories of what their families had already done, it makes you wonder why they wanted to get out there to fight themselves. They already knew that the price of being a soldier was often death. Let's look at some of the stories of this war that the boys at VMI could already tell us.

✚ Donald Allen was a sixteen-year-old cadet in 1864. He had two brothers who had graduated from VMI before him. One had been killed in the fighting at Gaines' Mill in 1862. The second died at Gettysburg in July 1863. When he was accepted as a cadet at VMI in

Matriculation Register of Cadets

N°.	DATE OF ADMISSION	NAME	AGE	COUNTY OR TOWN	STATE
1	Dec 24. 1863	S. B. Dabney	16	Buck	Miss
2	"	Wyndham Kemper	18	Worcester	Va
13	Jany 1 1863	F. F. Kennard	17	Charlotte	"
4	" 2	H. J. Walton	18	Henrico	"
5	" 10	J. Kemper	16	Montgomery	Tenn.
6	" 14	Col. Preston	17	"	Va
7	" 15	F. A. James	16	Memphis	Tenn
8	" 16	Geo. Mayo	18	Bath	Va
9	" "	F. Erwin	18	"	"
10	" "	Wm. W. Scott	18	"	"
11	" "	A. L. Grace	18	Orange	"
12	" 19	Wm. A. Kirkhull	21	"	"
13	" "	B. W. Leckham	16	Pittsylvania	"
14	" 20	A. B. Kennard	16	Culpeper	"
15	" 21	Alex. Thurman	17	Orange	"

Matriculation Register showing the names of students who entered the school in July 1863. Notice the ages of the cadets. (Courtesy of Virginia Military Institute Archives.)

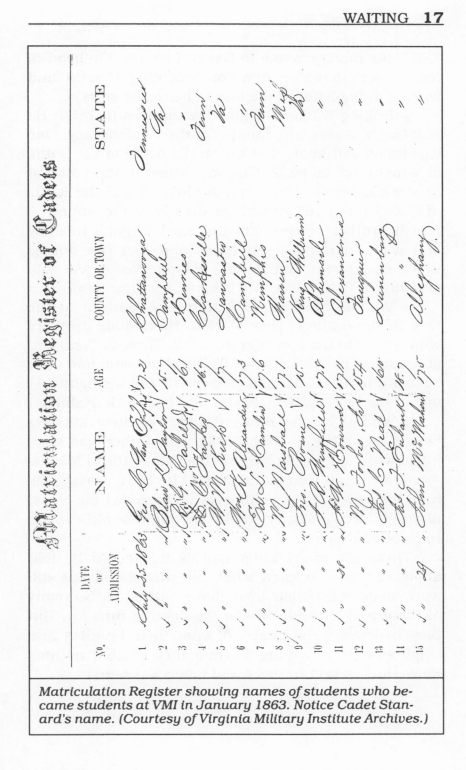

Matriculation Register showing names of students who became students at VMI in January 1863. Notice Cadet Stanard's name. (Courtesy of Virginia Military Institute Archives.)

1863, his mother wrote to General Smith, the head of the school, thanking him for accepting Donald and writing in the letter of the loss of her older sons.

✤ Bolling Walker Barton was eighteen in 1864. He had five brothers who fought for the Confederacy. One was killed within sight of his family home at the Battle of Winchester in 1862. One was killed in the battle at Fredericksburg in 1862. Another lost a leg at the Battle of Mine Run in 1863 and later died from the wound. A fourth brother served with the 33rd Virginia Infantry and was wounded seven times and had five horses killed under him. But Bolling Walker Barton was still studying at VMI so he could become a soldier, too.

✤ William Macfarland Patton was eighteen at the time of the Battle of New Market. He had six brothers who served in the Confederate army. Three of them had graduated from VMI. Two of his brothers who had once been students at VMI had already died in the fighting— one in the battle at Winchester and one at Gettysburg.

✤ William Norvell Radford turned eighteen six days before the Battle of New Market. His father had been killed while leading a charge at the first Battle of Manassas (called Bull Run by the North) in 1861, leaving behind his wife and eight children. William was the oldest of the children and now, finally, he would be old enough to go off and fight.

There are many other stories that could be told about cadets who knew what war was about, but still were anxious for their own chance at battle. So many of them had lost relatives in the fighting thus far. But they believed so strongly in what their families and neighbors were fighting for that they wanted nothing more than to get out there and fight themselves.

✤

Cadet Andrew Pizzini, Jr. was one of the many cadets who had his picture taken in his uniform when a photographer visited VMI. (Courtesy of Virginia Military Institute Archives.)

Several of the cadets at VMI were students there because they had already been involved in the fighting, but had been pulled from the army and sent to VMI where it was felt they would be safe. Here are the stories of six of the cadets who had already seen battle.

✠ John Cabell Early was serving in the Confederate army at age thirteen, carrying food and supplies to the fighting soldiers. He was at the first Battle of Manassas in 1861. At age fifteen he had served as a courier — a person who carries messages during battle — at the Battle of Gettysburg. His uncle, General Jubal Early, had sent him home to keep him away from the fighting.

✠ John Horsely enlisted in the army at sixteen without getting his mother's permission. He fought at the Battle of Fredericksburg, then his mother had him discharged from the army and sent to school at VMI.

✠ William Henry Cabell was enrolled by his parents at VMI in January 1862 when he had just turned sixteen years old. The following June, while he was home from VMI on sick leave, he snuck away and joined his brother, who was an officer in the Virginia infantry serving under General A. P. Hill. He fought with his brother in a battle near Richmond and even participated in a bloody charge that won the battle for the Confederacy. After the battle, he did not want to return to VMI but his parents, who had not given him permission to go off and fight, insisted he return to school.

✠ Samuel Houston Letcher left home to fight at age fifteen and fought in the trenches around Richmond. At the time of the Battle of New Market, he was still only sixteen years old. His father was the Governor of Virginia during the Civil War period. He had become a cadet at VMI on February 29, 1864, so he had only been a part of the cadet corps for a little over two months at the time of the battle.

✚ Charles Carter Randolph went off to war at age sixteen and served as a courier to General "Stonewall" Jackson at the second battle of Manassas and at Antietam. General J.E.B. Stuart was to remember him as "a young lad [who] . . . brought me several messages from General Jackson under circumstances of great personal peril and delivered his dispatches with great clearness and intelligence." Jackson was worried about him since he always took terrible risks to get his messages through and arranged for him to become a cadet at VMI. He also took great chances in the Battle of New Market.

✚ Thomas Herbert Shriver was another cadet who couldn't wait to get to war. Shriver fought at the Battle of Gettysburg in 1863 and also fought with the cavalry in northern Virginia. At Gettysburg, he served as a guide on the staff of General J.E.B. Stuart. Since he was still only seventeen, his commanding officers sent him to become a student at VMI.

✚

Cadets did have an important role to play in the Confederate army, even if it seemed boring to them. When the war had first started, VMI had been closed down and the students had gone to fight in the early battles. But General Lee and other Confederate generals soon realized that they would need trained officers if this war was going to last a long time. So in January 1862, the school was reopened. The cadets at VMI were there to learn about strategy, tactics, and leadership. When they graduated they would serve as the army's officers, and train and lead all of the soldiers who fought for the Confederacy.

The cadets did get a chance to leave VMI occasionally and serve as reserve troops when they were needed. General "Stonewall" Jackson had included the

Cadet John S. Wise would later write one of the best accounts of the cadets in the Battle of New Market. (Courtesy of Virginia Military Institute Archives.)

cadet corps in his campaign in the Shenandoah Valley in 1862. Several times in 1863 they were called out to assist the army, but always just as escorts or in other "boring" jobs. They had never gotten the opportunity to actually participate in the fighting at a battle.

One of the VMI cadets wrote a book many years after the war. He talked about what it was like to be a student at VMI in 1863 and 1864. His name was John S. Wise and he said that the cadets were not happy when some of the Confederate troops who had been in battle gave the Corps of Cadets a flag they had captured. He wrote: "We felt ashamed of having flags captured for us by others." He tells about all of the boys writing letters home, begging their parents to let them go and fight. He tells about boys deliberately getting themselves in trouble at school so that they would be sent home and then could join the army. He also talks about the many nights when "I wondered if my time would ever come."

The letters of another cadet have been saved and you can read in his own words how he felt about going to fight. Cadet Stanard wrote to his mother on April 8, 1864: "I think I have been very obedient in remaining here as long as I have, and only done so because I hated to go contrary to the wish of a fond and devoted Mother. I think Mother might very willingly give her consent now, that the prospect of the war ending soon is very great." His mother did not give her permission. But he would not need his mother's consent after all. In the end he would not only go against his mother's wishes but he would also disobey an order to stay behind with the supply wagons during the battle. In the end, he would pay the ultimate price for disobeying that order.

Finally, at the end of all their waiting, the time had come!

The cadets of the Virginia Military Institute were going to war!

Virginia Military Institute
May the 9th 1864

My darling Mother

Here I am, no longer a freeman, but a prisoner within the lofty walls of the V.M.I. I reached here safely, on Friday, evening, and it has been a source of regret to me ever since, that I should have been goose enough to leave when I did, And have to leave my trunks behind, So much for not taking the advice of a wise man (Mr. Chapman), doubtless they told you at the village, about my being left by the train, I did not care myself, but I was afraid poor brother would swear himself to death about it, was the only reason which actuated me to proffer-ness, in ▓ turning some means of conveyance to take me to Gordonsville, And after all I did not get there in time to see him, but unfortunately, in time for the Staunton train, Plague on it! I wish it had left before

Letter from Cadet Stanard to his mother, May 9, 1864, after returning to school from leave: "Here I am, no longer a free-man, but a prisoner within the lofty walls of the VMI." (Courtesy of Virginia Military Institute Archives.)

Chapter 3

THE CALL TO BATTLE

M ay 10, 1864 was going to be a special day for the cadets at VMI. Exactly one year before, General Thomas J. "Stonewall" Jackson had died after being accidentally shot by his own troops during the battle at Chancellorsville. "Stonewall" Jackson had once been a teacher at VMI and was one of the greatest generals in the Confederate army. He had been famous for protecting the area called the Valley of Virginia. The cadets thought of Jackson as their favorite hero and on this May 10th, there was going to be a special ceremony in his memory at VMI. A special flag was being brought to VMI and the cadet corps would get to raise the flag. Not only that, but because it was such a special day, they were getting a whole day off from classes and drills. For the cadets, this was a great holiday. But this day was to hold an even more special surprise for them.

On May 2, 1864, the Superintendent of VMI, General Francis H. Smith, had written a letter to General Breckinridge. In it he told him that he was getting the cadets ready in case Breckinridge needed their help. He said he had 280 cadets at VMI and could send about 250 of them to fight. He told him that he was making sure VMI had all the supplies the cadets would

This is a picture of the VMI Cadet Barracks before the Civil War. (Courtesy of Virginia Military Institute Archives.)

would need—"ammunition, tents, knapsacks, shovels and picks." His cadets, he told Breckinridge, would "be prepared to march at a moment's notice." General Smith, called "Old Specs" by the cadets (but only when he could not hear them), also kept the boys drilling and marching so that they would be ready when the time came. All of his planning was about to be used.

✠

These jackets are original jackets of the type worn by the cadets at VMI during the Civil War. These are kept in the VMI Museum at Lexington. (Courtesy of Virginia Military Institute Archives.)

At the end of the ceremonies on May 10th, the cadets went to bed. At ten o'clock they were awakened by "the long roll." This was a drum roll that called for them to line up in ranks on the parade grounds to receive orders. Many of them thought they were being called out for a surprise drill and they were not happy about it. After all, this had been their day off. It would be a mean trick if they had to drill tonight. They all lined up on the parade grounds and watched their commander talking with some officers. Finally he announced their orders to them. They were to prepare to leave in the morning to march to Staunton to join up with General Breckinridge's troops. A large group of Union soldiers was coming through the Valley and they were needed to help the small Confederate forces stop the invasion.

John Wise wrote in his book thirty-three years later that the boys listened to the news in total silence. Then they listened some more as they were given the list of things they would need to get ready—their canteens, their blankets, and their haversacks. Some of the boys were told that they were in charge of getting the ammunition together. Others needed to gather the food rations they would need for the march. When all of the instructions were given, suddenly, from all the boys came the sound of "wild cheering at the thought that our hour had come at last." The cadets of the Virginia Military Institute would finally get a chance to fight.

Chapter 4

THE MARCH DOWN THE VALLEY

The cadets had a busy night getting ready to march. Not only did they have a lot of work to do to get ready for the next day, but they were also so excited about what was going to happen that many of them could not sleep anyway.

The boys ate their breakfast by candlelight and then filled their haversacks with the leftover food. By sunrise, 264 of them were lined up and ready to go. John Wise says that they cheered as they marched out of the school grounds.

Of course, not all of the cadets were allowed to go. Watching the others leave was the group of twenty-seven cadets who were left behind to guard VMI. You can imagine how miserable and disappointed they must have felt as they watched their friends march away. One of them even cried and begged to go with them when he found out he was one of the ones who had to stay behind. Cadet Mark Hankins, who was one of the ones left to guard the school, would write forty-five years later that "It was at the time, and always will be a source of regret that I was in the detail left in Lexington to guard Barracks when the Corps marched away." Many years after the battle, when all of the cadets who fought at the battle were given medals, the group of cadets who stayed at VMI got medals too, because everyone knew that they really wanted to be on the battlefield fighting with their friends.

As the cadets begin their march, we have to talk about "up" and "down" in the Shenandoah Valley. Usually when we talk about someone going "up" to a place, we mean that they are going north. Going "down" a valley is usually going south. But the Shenandoah Valley is different. When the first settlers came into the Valley, they came south from Pennsylvania. But when they moved farther south and into the unknown, they always talked of this as moving "up" the Valley. This backwards way of talking about the Valley stuck and that is still how people talk about it today. So the cadets, marching north, were going "down" the Shenandoah Valley. The Union soldiers, marching south, were coming "up" the Shenandoah Valley. If you look at the following map, it should all make sense.

The Superintendent of VMI, General Francis H. Smith, had promised General Breckinridge that he would have the cadets in Staunton on May 12th. General Smith couldn't go with them because he was sick. He put the Commandant of Cadets, Colonel Scott Shipp, in charge of getting the cadets there in time. Colonel Shipp was only twenty-four years old at the time of the battle—not much older than the cadets he would be commanding. He had himself graduated from VMI in 1859 and he was a Latin teacher there in 1864.

Colonel Shipp had the cadets march eighteen miles on that first day. This was where all that drill and practice the cadets had been doing paid off. The road they marched on was hot and dusty and many of them had bad blisters on their feet by the end of the day. They camped for the night at the town of Midway.

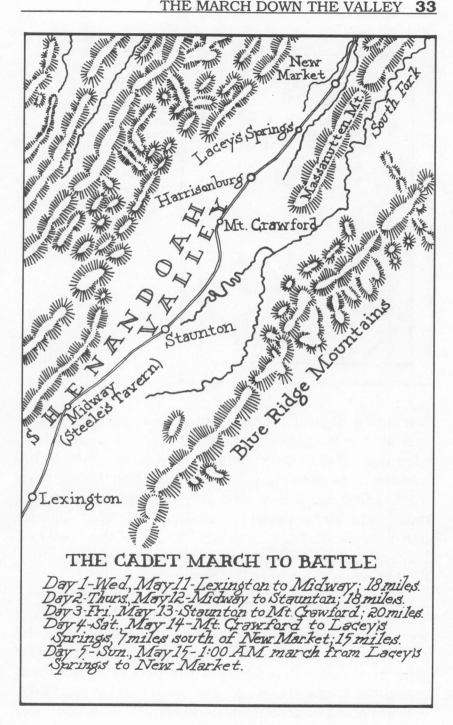

THE CADET MARCH TO BATTLE

Day 1-Wed., May 11-Lexington to Midway; 18 miles.
Day 2-Thurs., May 12-Midway to Staunton; 18 miles.
Day 3-Fri., May 13-Staunton to Mt. Crawford; 20 miles.
Day 4-Sat., May 14-Mt. Crawford to Lacey's
  Springs, 7 miles south of New Market; 15 miles.
Day 5-Sun., May 15-1:00 AM march from Lacey's
  Springs to New Market.

Because of the illness of General Smith, this twenty-four-year-old VMI graduate led the cadets at New Market. Scott Shipp would be wounded during the fighting in the orchard just past the Bushong House. (Courtesy of Virginia Military Institute Archives.)

During the night it started raining, and the rain continued all the next day as they finished their march to Staunton. One of the cadets wrote a letter home to his mother from Staunton. He told her that the eighteen mile march on the second day took place on roads that "were awful perfect loblolly all the way and we had to wade through like hogs." Three of the boys had blisters so bad from the march that they had to stay behind when the others left Staunton.

When they joined up with some of the troops in Staunton, the cadets found that a lot of the soldiers were not happy to see them. Many of them thought the cadets would not be able to fight. Cadet Royster would later remember that some of the people in Staunton called out to the Cadets as they marched by: "Ah! boys you are going to hear the bull dogs bark now." Some of

Letter from Cadet Stanard to his mother, May 12, 1864, from Staunton, telling her of their march: "the roads were awful perfect loblolly all the way and we had to wade through like hogs." (Courtesy of Virginia Military Institute Archives.)

the Confederate soldiers even started singing "Rock-a-bye Baby" when they marched by. That made the cadets very angry.

At 6:00 A.M. on Friday, May 13, 1864, General Breckinridge's army began its march. With the cadets added to his forces, his army now had 3,500 infantry and 248 artillery troops with twelve cannons. When these forces joined up with General Imboden at New Market, they would have about 1,500 more soldiers. They marched twenty miles, stopping just south of Harrisonburg. It was yet another day of marching in heavy rain.

On Saturday they started their march at 5:00 A.M., still in heavy rain. This time they marched about fifteen miles to a town called Lacey's Springs, which was only about seven miles from New Market.

As they camped for the night, for the first time the cadets could see the campfires of their enemy. They even had a chance to see some Union prisoners. As they set up camp they also saw a steady stream of people heading up the Valley to get away from New Market. The cadets knew that the Confederate army Breckinridge's troops had been marching to catch up with was now just ahead of them. They also knew that this waiting army, led by General John D. Imboden (whose brother was one of the cadets), had already had a few small skirmishes with the Union troops. By now, the cadets knew that tomorrow they would finally get their chance to fight.

Chapter 5

THE BATTLE

The cadets' sleep was not to last long on this night before their big battle. John Wise had guard duty that night. A little past midnight a horse came riding up the road. It was a messenger for Colonel Shipp. The cadets were "to march immediately, without beat of drum and as noiselessly as possible."

Colonel Shipp sent John Wise to wake up the cadets, and when they were lined up in their four companies the way they had been trained, the Colonel gave them their orders. Then Captain Frank Preston began to talk to them.

Before we see the cadets march into battle, we need to know some facts about Captain Preston. How well the cadets would fight on this day would depend on the training that he had given them. Captain Preston was not a VMI graduate. He had gone to school at Washington College (called Washington and Lee University today), which was located right next to VMI in Lexington. When the Civil War started, Frank Preston went off to fight. In one of the battles at Winchester, he was hit by a minié ball. His arm was so badly injured that the doctors had to amputate it. While he was still in the hospital, the Union troops captured Winchester and he was taken prisoner. Once he had recovered from his wound, he managed to escape from the hospital and get back to the Confederate army. Without his arm, he couldn't fight, but he still wanted to do something to help the Confederate cause. So he was asked to teach military tactics at VMI. The cadets whom he taught remembered him as a good teacher but also a tough one. As the cadets went into battle at New Market, he would be leading Company "B". But this morning before they marched, he wanted to talk to all of his students. John Wise remembered later that he talked "of home, of father, of mother, of country, of victory and defeat, of life, of death, of eternity." And then, with many of the boys in tears, he prayed with them that God would take care of them as they went into battle.

The cadets, now very serious and probably more than a little scared, left their camp at just after one o'clock in the morning. They marched six miles on the muddy Valley Turnpike towards New Market. The march took a long time because several times they had to stand by the side of the road and just wait— once in the middle of a heavy rain storm. At one of the breaks they stopped to cook and eat their breakfast.

When they marched past another brigade that was stopped and eating their breakfast, they heard some more of the teasing they had been getting ever since Staunton. This time the teasing helped to cheer them up. John Wise, who was getting a little bit scared by this time, said that the older troops seemed "as merry, nonchalant, and indifferent to the coming fight as if it were their daily occupation" (which, of course, it was). That helped the cadets feel that maybe it wouldn't be too bad to go into battle.

✛

It wasn't until mid-morning that they arrived at the place where General Breckinridge wanted them to line up. They went into position in the reserve lines, about one mile south of New Market itself, behind a rail fence near Shirley's Hill. General Breckinridge himself came to talk with Colonel Shipp. Later, Colonel Shipp wrote in his official report on the battle that General Breckinridge "informed me that he did not wish to put the Cadets in if he could avoid it, but that should occasion require it, he would use them very freely." When General Breckinridge stopped to talk to the cadets as he left, they cheered him.

The cadets settled into their positions and got ready for battle, filling their canteens and taking off their coats and haversacks so they would be ready to march quickly. For most of them the tension and excitement was incredible. They could now hear the fighting as the skirmishes continued but they still couldn't SEE anything. There is one funny story about a cadet who wasn't excited at all right then. Cadet George Lee, whose father was General Robert E. Lee's brother, fell asleep behind the rail fence, too tired to stay awake after the long march. Maybe his uncle had told him that real soldiers try to sleep whenever and wherever they can!

In this time just before the battle began, four of the cadets disobeyed a direct order—the only time all day when the cadets did not do what they were told to do. Cadets John Wise and Jack Stanard, along with two other cadets, were told that when the other cadets marched forward, they would have to stay behind with the supply wagons. They were not happy about this order. They abandoned the supply wagons and snuck back with the other cadets. No one was going to stop them from fighting now that they were so close. For Cadet Stanard it was one of the last decisions he would ever make.

✚

The time was 11:00 A.M. on Sunday, May 15, 1864. General Breckinridge had hoped to get the Union forces to attack him because he was in a good defending position and he knew that they had more troops than he did. But only skirmishes had taken place all morning. It looked like Union General Sigel was just going to sit there and not move his men. It was time for action. General Breckinridge gave the orders for the Confederate army, now about 6,200 strong since it joined up with General Imboden's troops, to begin the attack. As Colonel Shipp ordered the cadet corps forward and their flag bearer, Cadet Oliver Perry Evans, raised their flag, John Wise says, "every cadet leaped forward . . . thrilling with the consciousness that this was war."

As the Confederate troops marched forward, General Breckinridge stayed with his plan to keep the cadets as a reserve unit. Colonel Shipp reported that his orders were "to take position, after the deployment [of the regular troops] should have been made, 250 or 300 yards in rear of the front line of battle, and to maintain that distance." Right away, Shipp could see that the group of thirty-two cadets with their two cannon that made up the cadet artillery would not be able to keep up with the march because of the rough ground they would be crossing. So he sent that group to join up with the regular Confederate artillery on top of Shirley's Hill.

As part of Major McLaughlin's command, they spent an exhausting day. The artillery was in action the entire day, long before the infantry fighting began. The cadets who fought here would not have all the glory that came to the cadets who charged the Union

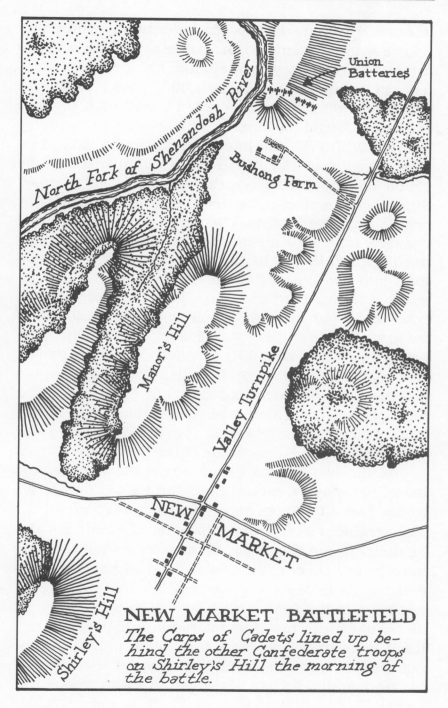

Union Batteries

North Fork of Shenandoah River

Bushong Farm

Manor's Hill

Valley Turnpike

NEW MARKET

Shirley's Hill

NEW MARKET BATTLEFIELD

The Corps of Cadets lined up behind the other Confederate troops on Shirley's Hill the morning of the battle.

lines at Bushong House that afternoon. But many people who have studied the battle say that it was the artillery that really won the battle for the whole Confederate army. Major McLaughlin would report to Colonel Shipp that he was very pleased with the way the cadets fought for him.

By 12:30 P.M. the lines had advanced to a place where they were starting to come within reach of the Union cannon fire. Here they stopped and Colonel Shipp again met with General Breckinridge to get his orders for the cadets. General Breckinridge had changed his mind about how he wanted his troops lined up. He divided his infantry (troops marching on foot) into two lines of about 1,600 soldiers each. Instead of having the cadet corps in back of the lines in reserve, he put them in as part of the second line of troops. The first line was made up of Wharton's brigade and the second line, which the cadets joined, was made up of Echols' brigade. The cadets would now be involved in the fighting, but hopefully in the most protected position. The second line would march "250 paces" [yards] behind the first line, and the cadets were at the far left side of the line.

As the two armies came into battle for the first time that day, General Breckinridge's Confederate troops had 4,087 men and eighteen guns [cannon]. He had another 1,200 troops made up of cavalry, which he didn't use in this battle because they would have to have been dismounted for this kind of fighting. General Sigel's Union army had 6,273 men and twenty-two guns in the field, with 1,700 additional men kept in reserve near by. General Breckinridge knew that this Union army had more men than he had. At one point in the morning before the armies met, he had his troops march back and forth to make it look like he had three full lines of troops. It is interesting to look back and learn that General Breckinridge's trick worked since General Sigel reported that the Confederate army he was facing had at least 9,000 men fighting that day.

✠

The Confederate troops moved forward. With Wharton's line moving toward them, the Union guns started firing their artillery at them. They couldn't get their aim just right so the first line was not badly hit. By the time the second line (which the cadets were part of) got to the same place, the Union shells were falling right where they were marching. For the first time the cadet corps came under fire. Colonel Shipp later said in his report that "Great gaps were made through the ranks but the cadet, true to his discipline, would close in to the center to fill the interval and push steadily forward."

The cadets continued marching like this for about a quarter mile on open ground, closing their ranks as they saw their friends shot down around them. Four of the cadets would die in this open field. Their friends who had been hit were left behind as the line kept moving forward. Union soldiers, watching them advance, could not figure out who these soldiers were, in their neat uniforms that were so different from the ones the regular army wore. Later on, when they found out that the troops marching at them so steadily and proudly had been the cadets, they would say that the cadets had marched as if they were on parade.

Ahead and to the right of the cadets the troops of the 62nd Virginia Regiment and the 1st Missouri Regiment (part of Wharton's brigade) were being cut to pieces as they came out around a house that was between the lines and the Union artillery batteries. Some of the

This photo of the Bushong House was taken in 1880, but the house looked the same as it had at the time of the battle. (Courtesy of Virginia Military Institute.)

books say that sixty out of sixty-five of the men in the
1st Missouri were killed or wounded. Others say only
two out of every three men died or were injured in this
regiment. Either way, these troops suffered very heavy
casualties and it became time for them to be pulled
back before all of them were killed. As these soldiers
pulled back, they left a gap right in the center of the
Confederate line. General Breckinridge now had to
make the decision he had not wanted to make. His assistant, Major Semple, advised him to send in the
cadets: "General, why don't you put the cadets in line?
They will fight as well as our men." General Breckinridge hesitated and said ". . . they are only children
and I cannot expose them to such fire as our center
will receive." But there really was no other choice that
could be made. The official accounts all say that with
tears in his eyes, Breckinridge gave the order, "Put the
boys in . . . and may God forgive me."

The cadets were moved forward into the gap, split-
ting into two groups to go around the Bushong house,
with Company A and Company B going to the right
and Company C and Company D going to the left. On
the other side of the house they found themselves in
an orchard only 200 yards or so from the Union batteries.

Colonel J. Stoddard Johnston, aide to General
Breckinridge during the battle, would write later of
what the cadets faced as they moved into position:
"Our troops had reached the summit of the slope and,
between them and the enemy's line, was a level, unob-
structed pasture, across which they had to march,
under a terrific fire of artillery and musketry. Here occurred the heaviest loss of the day. The cadets suffered severely." As the cadet corps moved through the
orchard, cadets started being hit at a terrible rate.
Many of the cadets killed or wounded fell at this spot.

Then Colonel Shipp himself fell, with a shell fragment hitting his shoulder. Captain Henry Wise took command and ordered the cadets to lie down behind an open rail fence about four feet high at one side of the orchard.

From this position the cadets had their first chance all day to fire on the enemy. Before, all they could do was keep marching as the Union cannon balls burst around them. Now they were finally close enough to fire back. The cadets huddled behind the fence as the bullets whizzed by them. In the middle of all the fighting, one thing did happen that the cadets would remember as very funny. Captain Henry Wise, crawling to the fence position, had a shell go past just above him. He wasn't injured but parts of his jacket and pants were shot away. Even he remembered later looking around desperately for "clothes enough to sit on." But even that funny memory would come long after the battle. Right now the cadets, for the first time all day, were getting scared. Their officers tried to calm them down. Captain Preston lay near the fence, lying on top of his one good arm to protect it, smiling and encouraging the cadets as they lay under this terrible rain of bullets. As time went on and they had been there for almost thirty minutes, the boys became more and more scared.

There were really only two choices that could be made—they could fall back or they could charge. With Colonel Shipp wounded the decision had to be made by Captain Henry Wise. He would say later that he was afraid that if the cadets stayed where they were for even a few more minutes, they would lose their courage. He also thought that if they all fell back, they would lose as many cadets under the cannon fire as they would if they charged.

Henry Wise made his decision. The command was

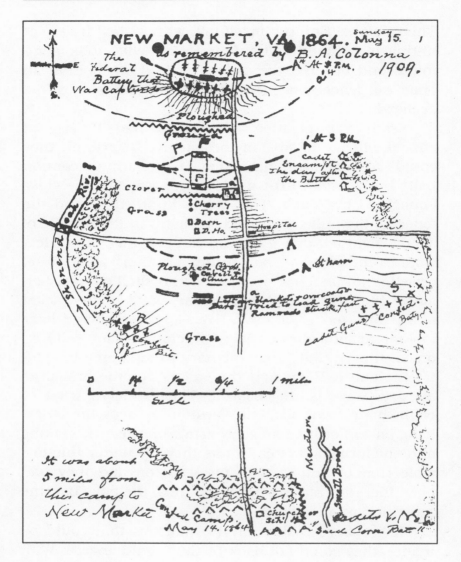

Cadet Benjamin A. Colonna's map of the battlefield. (Courtesy of Virginia Military Institute Archives.)

"Charge." The cadets, as one remembered later, "rose as a man, got over the fence, and moved forward across the field straight for the enemy's guns." Getting to the Union battery was not going to be easy. Between the orchard and the battery was a field of plowed ground that was the Bushong farm's wheat field. It was about fifty yards wide—half the length of a football field. Because of all the rain, the field had turned into a sea of mud. And on top of it all, it was pouring rain again now. The cadets, in charging, put themselves in front of the other Confederate lines. When the others saw their charge, they joined them. The whole line moved forward, ignoring all the bullets being fired at them. The boys found themselves stuck knee deep in the mud. Many of them found their shoes and socks sucked right off their feet. As they slogged slowly across the field, they made easy targets for the Union troops. One cadet was hit seven times as he tried to cross the field. Cadet Randolph, the reckless cadet with battle experience, told the cadets with him not to try to avoid the bullets because "if a ball's going to hit you, it'll hit you anyway." Then he was hit and fell down. Today this wheat field is called the Field of Lost Shoes.

Many of the wounded from the 62nd Virginia and the 1st Missouri, lying on the field, would later say how great the cadets looked as they charged forward. Many of them cheered the boys as they struggled along. The story goes that one of the wounded tried to get to his feet to join the charge but was hit in the face and fell back to the ground.

The charge did not take long. After crossing the field the cadets surged up the hill to the Union battery. The battery commander, Captain Albert von Kleiser, knew he was defeated and tried to get his guns and men away. The cadets, reaching the top of the hill, captured one of the cannons and several Union prisoners.

The cadet corps split into two sections to come around the house in this picture. The Union battery was located at the spot from which this picture was taken. (Photo by W. Michael Beller.)

The fighting here became hand to hand. Many of the cadets remembered the sight of Cadet Hanna fighting a sword duel with a Union officer who would not surrender to him. Using only his cadet saber, he won!

✠

It was 6:30 P.M. The Union forces were on the run. The regular Confederate troops were chasing after the stragglers. The battle was over for the cadets. Cadet Benjamin Colonna remembered the scene as they reformed into ranks and General Breckinridge rode over to talk to them. "We presented arms, he raised his hat and said 'Young gentlemen, I have you to thank for the result of today's operations.' He then rode away followed by our cheers." As John Wise would write: "We had won a victory,—not a Manassas or an Appomattox, but, for all that, a right comforting bit of news went up the pike that night to General Lee."

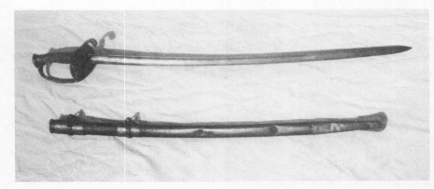

This sword, which belonged to Cadet Benjamin Colonna, is now in the collection at the New Market Battlefield Historical Park. (Photo by W. Michael Beller.)

Chapter 6

AFTER THE BATTLE

The fighting was over. The boys had proved themselves to be great soldiers. Four of the cadets were now dead. Another would die before the day ended. Five others were to die from the wounds they had received. And forty-five others had been wounded but would survive. When all the counting was done, almost one out of every four of them had been killed or wounded. This added up to a casualty rate of 24%. Except for the one company of the 1st Missouri Regiment, with a casualty rate of 64%, no other unit in the Battle of New Market suffered as many losses as the cadets did.

Dead on the battlefield were Sgt. Cabell, Pvt. Crockett, Pvt. Jones, and Pvt. McDowell.

✚ William Henry Cabell was eighteen years old and was the best student in his VMI class. He was a cousin of General Breckinridge and he went into battle side by side with his younger brother, Robert. It was not the first time he had gone into battle with one of his brothers. We heard about him in Chapter 2 when he ran away and fought with his older brother near Richmond. The brothers were separated during the fighting. After the battle, Robert tried to find his brother and instead found his body on the field. He and Crockett and Jones were all killed by one cannon

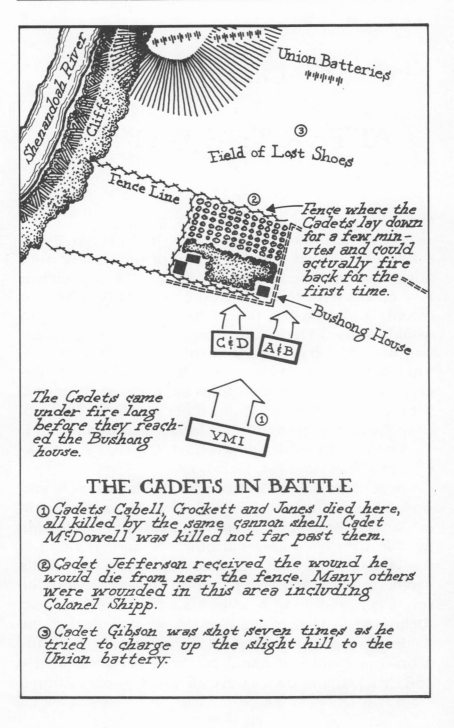

The Cadets came under fire long before they reached the Bushong house.

THE CADETS IN BATTLE

① Cadets Cabell, Crockett and Jones died here, all killed by the same cannon shell. Cadet McDowell was killed not far past them.

② Cadet Jefferson received the wound he would die from near the fence. Many others were wounded in this area including Colonel Shipp.

③ Cadet Gibson was shot seven times as he tried to charge up the slight hill to the Union battery.

Cadet Sergeant William H. Cabell, killed instantly at the Battle of New Market. (Courtesy of Virginia Military Institute Archives.)

shell. John Wise wrote in his book that "a blanket would have covered all three."

✤ Charles Gay Crockett was seventeen years old when he was killed by that same cannon shell. He had only been a student at VMI for fifteen weeks when he was killed. In the official report of the battle that was written a couple of days later, Captain Preston said the boys were only 400 yards from the Union lines when they were killed.

✤ Henry Jenner Jones, the third cadet killed by that shell, had turned seventeen only two months before the battle. His older brother had been killed in the

Cadet Jaqueline Beverly Stanard would disobey an order on the day of the battle and refuse to stay with the baggage wagons. It would be one of the last decisions he ever made. He told his roommate the night before the battle that he thought he was going to die in the battle. (Courtesy of Virginia Military Institute Archives.)

fighting at Seven Pines, Virginia. Another brother wrote to General Smith, the head of VMI the week after the battle, asking, on his mother's behalf, for "the manner of his death; where rests the body; and any other circumstances of his death that may be of interest to her in her double affliction."

✤ William Hugh McDowell, age seventeen, died not far past the first three. He had been killed when a bullet went through his heart. His father wrote in a letter two weeks after the battle: "Your letter informing me of the death of my son William McDowell has been received. It came upon me like a clap of Thunder in a clear sky as I was not aware the Cadets had been called out."

Not far away, in a battlefield hospital, Jaqueline Beverly Stanard, called Jack by his friends and Bev by his family, was dying. He was one of the older cadets and had celebrated his nineteenth birthday just a couple of weeks before the battle. He was the cadet who wrote to his mother from Staunton, telling her about wading "like hogs" in the rain on their march to Staunton. He was also one of the cadets who were supposed to stay with the supply wagons behind the lines during the battle. Jack Stanard was also John Wise's roommate at VMI. John Wise writes in his book that Jack told him the night before the battle that he was sure he was going to die in the battle. If you visit the battlefield at New Market today, you can see the letter he wrote from Staunton to his mother. You can also see the telegram that was sent announcing his death in the battle.

✚

Five other cadets would die from their battle wounds — one of them not until July 20th, over two months after the battle.

✚ Thomas Garland Jefferson, age seventeen, died on May 18th, three days after the battle. His great-grandfather was the brother of Peter Jefferson, the father of President Thomas Jefferson. His roommate, Moses Ezekiel—who would later design the monument at VMI to the cadets—found him and stayed with him until he died at the home of a family in New Market. In his cadet file at VMI is the letter from his father, dated

Thomas Garland Jefferson, a relative of President Thomas Jefferson, died three days after the battle from the wounds he received during the fighting. (Courtesy of Virginia Military Institute Archives.)

June 3, 1864, giving permission for his son's body to be removed to Lexington and reburied there in the VMI cemetery with the other cadets who died in the battle.

✦ Joseph Christopher Wheelwright, age seventeen, died on June 2, 1864, over two weeks after the battle. The cadets' own doctor, Colonel Madison, who stayed with the wounded cadets after the battle, sent in a report on June 1st. In it he said that Wheelwright was dying at the home of a doctor in Harrisonburg. They had tried to bring him back to VMI, but he was too badly injured. His father, writing to give permission for his son's body to be buried in the VMI cemetery, remembered that his son had desperately wanted to fight in the war. His brothers were all fighting in the Confederate army and he kept telling his parents that his school was like a prison to him. He ends his letter with "His parents fondly hoped that he, at least, might be kept out of danger, while his brothers were incurring all the risks and chances of war."

✦ Luther Cary Haynes, age nineteen, died in Richmond, Virginia, on June 15, 1864. He was wounded in the battle, but it was not a very serious wound. He went home to recuperate, but died there unexpectedly.

✦ Alva Curtis Hartsfield, age nineteen, died in Petersburg, Virginia, on June 26, 1864. He was not badly wounded in the battle. However, he caught the measles while the cadets were camped at Richmond the week after the battle. He seemed to be getting better and was given permission to go home until he recovered completely. On the way home, he became sick again and died. Cadet Colonna would write later that "He was not killed at New Market but he was a victim of that campaign as much as Cadet Atwill was."

✦ Samuel Francis Atwill, age eighteen, did not die until July 20, 1864, over two months after the battle. He

Cadet Samuel Atwill died from his wounds over two months after the battle. (Courtesy of Virginia Military Institute Archives.)

had been shot in the leg during the battle and was getting better at the home of a doctor in Staunton. Then he became sick with lockjaw, a very serious infection that many Civil War soldiers got because in those days, doctors didn't understand how important it was to keep all of their instruments clean and free of germs. Lockjaw was a terrible way to die, and the records say Cadet Atwill died the most painful death of all the cadets who died from New Market battle wounds.

Because he did not die until so long after the battle, there are letters in his file that he wrote after the battle. These are sad to read since you know that he

This is a photograph of a museum display of New Market memorabilia. Notice especially the rifle. The Curator of New Market Battlefield Park describes how it got this way: "The splintered Austrian rifle was carried into battle at New Market on May 15, 1864, by VMI Cadet Private Charles Henry Read, Jr. A Union shell burst near him, wounding him over the right eye. His rifle was knocked from his shoulder and its barrel bent at right angles by the tremendous force of the explosion." (Courtesy of Virginia Military Institute Archives.)

was going to die. He wrote to General Smith on July 3, 1864 asking for some money so that he could go to his home to finish recovering from his injury. He says that his "wound is doing very well, but gives me a great deal of pain some times." There is also a letter from his father to General Smith dated July 9th. He had just found out that his son was wounded and wanted to find out where his son was so he could go to see him. In the final letter, dated August 8th, his father writes to General Smith, telling him that he has just learned of his son's death, adding "It is painful to lose a child at home but to be unable to see him, was very greavious [his spelling] to me."

✚

Many other cadets were wounded but did not die from their wounds. John Wise was hurt when a cannon shell exploded right in front of his face. Four others were hurt by the same shell, including Captain A. Govan Hill, who was one of the cadets' tactics teachers at VMI and was leading Company C of the cadets in the battle. His skull was fractured by the shell, but he survived.

Cadet Captain Samuel Sprigg Shriver was shot and injured early in the battle when a piece of a shell went into his left elbow. He got back up and went back to the fighting. Then a musket ball hit him in the same elbow and he had to leave the field. His arm was stiff for the rest of his life.

Charles Carter Randolph, the cadet in Chapter 2 who was sent to VMI by Stonewall Jackson to get him away from the fighting because of all the risks he took, was also wounded in the battle. He lost his hearing in one ear from the wound. His older brother had died three days before in a battle near Richmond.

"Berry Hill"
Orange Ct-Ho
July 28th 1864.

Cadet L. C. Wise-

I scarcely know how to thank my dear young friend for his thoughtfull kindness, & beautiful tribute to the memory of our dear one, now sleeping under the shadows of his own Home!

'Tis true my dear friend no earthly consolation can be given to sooth entirely the heart sorrow we are all compelled to bear, but it is sweet & above all things comforting to hear his praises from those among whom he so lately dwelled-

Your name sounds like a household word- so often has it fallen from his dear lips- Indeed I feel as if I knew all his room-mates, & could call them Brother-

Most anxious were we to have

Letter received by John S. Wise in response to his letter offering condolences to the Stanard family on the death of Cadet Stanard. "Tis true my dear friend no earthly consolation can be given to sooth entirely the hearts sorrow we are all compelled to bear, but it is sweet & above all things comforting to hear his praises from those among whom he lately dwelled." (Courtesy of Virginia Military Institute Archives.)

One final story is that of Cadet Franklin Graham Gibson, age nineteen, who was wounded seven times during the battle. His brother, writing about his injuries later, said "Frank Gibson was 'shot to pieces' in the charge of the cadet corps at New Market . . . his leg was shattered below the knee. Another ball through his thigh. One through the hand, losing two fingers. Another in the cheek." When Colonel Madison, the cadet doctor, made his report on June 1, 1864, he was still really worried about whether Gibson would even live. But Gibson did live and later became a teacher and then a lawyer.

✛

In the Archives of VMI there are records of all of the cadets who were ever students at the Institute. Along with the records are documents that have been kept for important things that have happened at the school since it opened in 1839. Among all the papers there are three that date from May 1866. These are the bills

THE SOUTHERN TELEGRAPH COMPANIES.

Terms and Conditions on which Messages are Received by these Companies for Transmission

The public are notified that in order to guard against mistakes in the transmission of messages, every message of importance ought to be repeated by being sent back from the station at which it is to be received to the station from which it is originally sent. Half the usual price for transmission will be charged for repeating the message, and while these Companies will as heretofore use every precaution to insure correctness, they will not be responsible for mistakes or delays in the transmission or delivery of repeated messages beyond five hundred times the amount paid for sending the message, nor will they be responsible for mistakes or delays in the transmission of unrepeated messages, from whatever cause they may arise, nor the delays arising from interruptions in the workings of their Telegraphs, nor for any mistake or omissions of any other Company over whose lines a message is to be sent to reach the place of destination. All messages will hereafter be received by these Companies for transmission subject to the above conditions.

J. R. DOWELL, Gen'l Sup't, Richmond, Va.   W. S. MORRIS, Pres't, Richmond, Va

Telegram of May 16, 1864: "Cadet Stanards body is at New Market I presume." (Courtesy of Virginia Military Institute Archives.)

These photographs show the front and back of the flag the cadets carried into battle. The original flag was cut into pieces and given out to all the cadets to keep it from being taken by the Union troops when they burned VMI. (Courtesy of Virginia Military Institute Archives.)

for the wagons and people that brought home to VMI the bodies of five of the cadets who were killed in the battle. VMI paid $121.75 to bring the cadets home to VMI.

There is another "after the battle" story to be told. The cadets who were not injured in the battle did not return to VMI right away. Instead, the cadet corps was marched to Charlottesville where they were sent by train to Richmond. Many of the cadets, who finally had gotten their wish to fight, would not go back to school. Instead they joined the regular Confederate army and fought in the trenches around Richmond. The rest of the cadets were marched back to VMI. No sooner had they settled back in than the orders came that a huge Union force was headed up the Valley. This time there was only a Confederate army of 2,000 men to stop them. The cadets fought with the army to try and stop the Union advance. But the Confederate army was forced to retreat, and the cadets received orders to leave VMI and retreat away from the Union army toward Lynchburg.

As they left VMI the boys cut up their battle flag into tiny pieces so each of them could have a piece and so that Union forces could not take it. Many of those pieces are now on display at the New Market Battlefield Historical Park, along with a reproduction of the original flag. On June 11, 1864, Union troops led by General David Hunter stopped at the Virginia Military Institute just long enough to burn all of its buildings.

If you visit VMI today you can see in the walls of the original barracks buildings three cannon shells that struck the walls and embedded themselves in it without exploding. The destruction by the Union troops was total and everything was lost — even the books in the library were all stolen or burned. Many people feel that the only reason this was done was because the Union troops were angry at having been defeated at New Market by BOYS.

This is what the cadet barracks at VMI looked like after the school was burned by Union General Hunter in June 1864. (Courtesy of Virginia Military Institute Archives.)

Chapter 7

AFTER THE WAR

The Civil War finally came to an end on April 9, 1865, almost one year after the Battle of New Market. Many of the cadets fought with the Confederate armies in the closing days of the long war. For one of the former cadets, the end of the war came one day too late. Cadet George Seaborn, who had fought with the artillery section during the New Market battle, died in a battle at Dinwiddie Court House the day before the war ended.

The surviving cadets went on with their lives. Many were successful businessmen. They became lawyers, farmers, bankers, teachers, doctors, clergymen, and engineers. Cadet Charles Faulkner became a U.S. Senator from West Virginia; John S. Wise served in the U.S. Congress from Virginia and was a candidate for Governor of Virginia at one time; Cadet Thomas Hayes became the Mayor of Baltimore, Maryland; Cadet Andrew Pizzini, Jr. became a businessman who set up the first successful electric street railway company in the world; Cadet Moses Ezekiel went on to become a world famous sculptor. In time he would design a monument to honor his fellow cadets, including his roommate, who did not survive the battle.

These five cadets, all of whom had fought at New Market, posed together for a photograph a couple of years after the battle. In the front row (left to right) are Cadet Edward M. Tutwiler, Cadet John L. Tunstall, and Cadet Thomas G. Hayes. In the back row are Cadet Hardaway H. Dinwiddie and Cadet Gaylord B. Clark. (Courtesy of Virginia Military Institute Archives.)

As successful as they were to become, for many of the cadets, their fight at New Market would always be to them the most important thing that had happened in their lives. Forty years after the battle, the VMI Alumni Association decided to present a "Cross of Honor" to each of the cadets who had been part of the Corps of Cadets on May 15, 1864, including those who had had to stay behind or were home on leave during the battle. All the cadets who were still living were invited to the ceremony to receive their medals. Medals for cadets who had died were given to their nearest relative. That ceremony brought many of the cadets together for the first time since the class had split up after the burning of VMI.

✛

The fact that the cadets had gone on to lead their own busy lives, sometimes far away from VMI and the people they had known there, did not lessen their strong feelings about their part in the Battle of New Market. Just over fifty years after the battle, the man who had commanded the 62nd Virginia Infantry, the troops that fought alongside the cadets, wrote an article for *The Confederate Veteran*. In the article he said he thought that the cadets had not really been that important to the battle, and that all they did was cover ground that his troops had already cleared of Union troops. He also felt that the cadets had gotten all of the praise and glory while the other regular Confederate troops involved in the battle were ignored.

The reaction of the surviving cadets was tremendous. Captain Henry Wise wrote a letter to all of them asking them to write down their recollections of the battle. He also asked for comments from officers in both the Union and Confederate armies. If you go to the

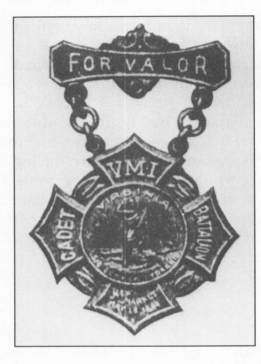

The "Cross of Honor" was awarded to all of the cadets who were members of the Corps of Cadets at the time of the battle. (Courtesy of Virginia Military Institute Archives.)

Archives at the VMI Library today, you can spend hours reading the letters that the cadets wrote back telling what they remembered about the battle that had taken place over fifty years before.

The letters are very interesting reading because they capture the memories of the actual people who were there. Obviously there is no way to include more than just a few of their comments here. But the ones I have included seemed to best represent how all of the cadets felt looking back on this important day in their lives.

Cadet Francis L. Smith, a successful attorney and former member of the Virginia State Senate, wrote: "I remember distinctly the fact of our lying down in this position, because I was immediately next to Captain Preston, who having lost one of his arms at the first Battle of

Manassas, protected the other as well as he could by keeping it under his body . . . At any rate, the order to 'Fire' was given, and as above narrated, I was wounded at the very moment the volley was being fired . . . I was placed upon the horse which Cooney Ricketts had ridden . . . and taken from the battle field."

Cadet Gideon A. Davenport ran an insurance company and later was a banker. He remembered: "About this time we passed a group of wounded soldiers, who cheered us, but a shell, intended for us, burst in their midst, and they were silent . . . The rain was falling in torrents and the smoke obscured our view—the noise was deafening . . . The Cadets within ten or fifteen minutes had lost more than forty killed or wounded . . . In a charge at the double quick Cadet Lieut John Hanna, in a hand to hand fight, captured a horse from an orderly who was attempting to escape from our fire."

Cadet Thomas W. Wilson, a bookkeeper in the years after the Civil War, wrote: "Just after passing the house my new rod got stuck in my gun. When Redwood said throw it away and pick up another which I did. I have often thought that I picked McDowells gun as it was here he was instantly killed within a few feet of me . . . It was here that my roommate childhood friend & life long friend Wm White of A Co. got his fearful wound with a grape shot which struck him just below the hip joint and shattered the bone."

Cadet Nelson B. Noland, a civil engineer and farmer, remembered: "As we descended the slope in front of us, Capt. A. G. Hill, of C Co., was wounded, as well as several others in my company; and here for the first time it occurred to me that maybe we were not 'Playing soldier' this time . . . The fire was furious at this time . . . I believed I was bound to get killed . . . Whilst lying there with the air literally filled with Yankee missiles, each one of which seemed to miss me only by

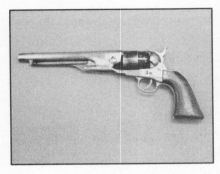

This pistol is called "Chatterin Sal" and was carried in the battle by Cadet J.J. Reid. It is part of the collection at the VMI Museum in Lexington. (Courtesy of Virginia Military Institute Archives.)

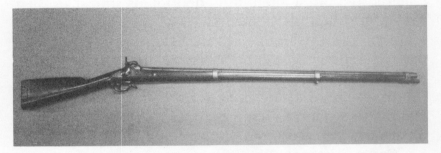

Cadet John S. Wise carried this rifle in the battle. It is on display at the VMI Museum. (Courtesy of Virginia Military Institute Archives.)

a scant sixteenth of an inch . . . I saw them falling like jackstraws, on their backs, faces, sides and knees . . . Up to this time I had not seen a Yankee, to know him, and rushed ahead with the balance as fast as I could, looking for something to shoot at."

Cadet James B. Baylor, later a civil engineer, would look back and say: "I remember, that the mud was terrific, as we advanced . . . We were exposed to such a fire, at this time, that, if we had long remained in this position we would have been almost exterminated."

Cadet Samuel B. Adams, writing from the mine he owned in Arizona, reminisced: "The enemy had our range and was giving us grape and canister with all their might and main. It was a hot place. I remember very well as we came into this little field one of my shoes came off and I had to turn around and pull it out of the mud and put it on again and it seemed to me I was a long time doing it."

What Cadet Lawrence Royster remembered most was results of the battle: "Returning over the field after the fight I saw a musket sticking up by the body of Cabell, a ball had struck him in the breast on his pocket knife, which was broken, but did not reach the flesh . . . Stanard received five balls in his leg near the knee. Randolph was shot in the cheek, the ball coming out behind the ear; he could not speak, but told us afterwards that he heard some one distinctly say, 'Oh! he cannot live'; but he recovered."

Cadet David G. Mohler, involved in real estate as an adult, recalled: "Here Capt. Henry A. Wise took command, and, with very emphatic adjectives, advised what he wanted given the Yankees . . . I well remember a Cadet (Bransford, I think), lying by my side, having a splinter from a rail in front driven into the back of his hand by a grape shot passing that way."

Cadet John W. McGavock, owner of large tracts of grazing land in later years, remembers the same scene Cadet Davenport did: "I recollect seeing far in advance of us a gallant confederate, he was half reclining, evidently wounded. He was cheering all he could with one hand and voice. Holding himself up with the other. I saw many a bullet strike him and he was perfectly still when we passed him . . . I was within a few feet of Cabell & Crockett & _____ [Jones] when they were killed yet I knew nothing about it [until] the battle was over."

When Captain Wise asked the cadets to send their recollections of the battle, Cadet Porter Johnson, a farmer in Wheeling, West Virginia, sent him twenty-three pages of memories. It is one of the most detailed letters in the whole file. He writes: "The whole picture is as distinct before me as if it were yesterday. Of late years there seems to be a feeling of jealousy on the part of other commands towards the cadets. Some evidently think we are getting to much credit and praise and others not enough . . . After crossing this ravine we struck the soft wheat field where some of the boys lost their shoes. From this point it was all up a gentle slope to the crest where the Battery was placed. I don't believe there could have been, just then a more accurate firing than those men did . . . Here I was turned clear around my gun flew over my head I never saw it again at least to recognize it as the one I had carried. One piece struck just over the heart—a great rent was torn in my jacket and shirt and the skin cut, I happened to have in the pocket of my jacket 2 army crackers some letters and a hankerchief. And I verily believe these broke the blow so as to save my life but another piece struck me on the arm. My first impression was that my arm was torn off at the shoulder . . . There lay poor Stanard the worst shot up man I ever saw. Then poor Cable [Cabell] and my own roommate Crcket [Crockett] with the back part of his head shot away . . . Oh, it was pittifull."

Cadet Henry C. Bowen, a lumber dealer in Virginia, remembers something funny from the battle: "I remember well when you lost your coat-tail & the seat of your trousers and Lewis Wimbush gave you a pair of Yankey trousers . . . I look back with pleasure & sometimes think it was the happiest part of my life, to be associated with some of the noblest men of the South."

Cadet George T. Lee, nephew of General Robert E. Lee, who went to sleep while waiting for battle, gives a very clear account of the entire battle that includes his thoughts at the time: "A sight, which impressed itself on me during this advance, was that of a Confederate soldier lying wounded on the ground, and who seemed to have a great piece torn out of his side by a shell. The sight was distressing, sickening and scary, and made me quite dread what I expected to have to pass through . . . We then went past the house and got into the orchard, where canister and other missiles were raining like hail. It seemed impossible for men to pass through such a storm . . . when ordered to rise and go forward, I felt that we were about to get in some work of our own—to do something to the fellows in front of us; an eagerness to get at it came over my spirit, all thought of the danger around passed away . . . I wiped the mud off my gun as well as I could, dropped on one knee, rested my elbow on the other and fired. I had a heavy old Belgian musket . . . and I could not take aim . . . without a rest; so I used my left knee as a rest for my left elbow, and aimed, so well as I could, at the brass buckles on the belts of the enemy."

One final recollection for this chapter cames from Colonel Theodore F. Lang, a member of the staff of General Sigel, the Union troop commander at the battle. He remembers looking through his field glasses and: "I beheld an unfamiliar sight for a battle field. A body of several hundred, with bright uniforms, shining swords with polished buttons, and hadsom [handsome] flags as if just come from the manufacturers, kept the alignment perfect . . . I must say that I never witnessed a more gallant advance and final charge than was given by those brave boys on that field. They fought like veterans, nor did the dropping of their comrades by the ruthless bullet deter them from their mission, but on, on they came."

Chapter 8

VMI AND THE BATTLEFIELD TODAY

Most people today, looking back at a battle that happened over 125 years ago, know that the cadets did not win the Battle of New Market all by themselves. They also realize that the cadets did play an important part in winning the battle. At a moment in time, at an important place in the Confederate line, they did what any well-trained and seasoned soldier would have done—they fought bravely and died gallantly. Their glory comes not from having won the victory single-handedly without the rest of the Confederate army. Instead it comes from having done exactly what they had been trained to do, and having done it very well. And for boys, aged fifteen to nineteen, most of whom had never fought before, fighting as well as seasoned soldiers did was glory enough.

The myth that developed over the years about the cadets only takes away from the reality of the good, solid job they did. Their conduct and bravery under fire stand alone. All the issues that have arisen in the time since the battle, whether the cadets actually captured a Union battery and whether they charged while the regular Confederate army held back and whether the regular Virginia troops had already cleared the field for them—all of these really do not matter. What does matter is that the cadets did exactly what they had been telling the adults in their world—their parents, teachers, etc.—they could do. They could and did fight in a battle with courage and bravery.

✤

The VMI cadets were not even the only cadet corps to fight for the Confederacy during the Civil War. The Corps of Cadets from the University of Alabama also saw action. The Alabama cadets, known as the "Katydids," helped to protect their capital city of Selma from attack by Union forces in July 1864. These cadets were actually younger than the cadets from VMI —most of them were only fifteen and sixteen years old. Unlike the VMI cadets, they never had a chance to take part in a real battle. But as part of the Confederate army, they served well to hold off the capture of Selma by Union troops in 1864. The following year, like the VMI cadets, they had to watch their school be burned down by the invading Union troops when Tuscaloosa, Alabama was taken by the Union armies.

Most historians agree that VMI was important to the Confederacy during the Civil War. But these historians do not say that it was because of the Battle of New Market. VMI was nicknamed the "West Point of the Confederacy." It was important because of the people who had graduated from VMI or taught there and were fighting as the officers in the Confederate army. General Thomas "Stonewall" Jackson is only the most famous of all these men. In a report General Francis Smith, Superintendent of VMI, made in 1865, he listed the former teachers at VMI who had been killed or wounded in battle. Four former VMI professors had died in battle and twelve others had been wounded. One source says that seventeen VMI graduates held the rank of general during the Civil War.

The cadets themselves had many relatives who had graduated from VMI and had fought or died for the Confederacy. Cadet Jacob Imboden knew that his brother, Captain Francis Imboden, of the VMI Class of 1864, was fighting not far away from him during the Battle of New Market. Cadet Donald Allen had two brothers who died during the war and were graduates of VMI. Cadets Coleman, Garnett, Harvie, and Hiden were among the cadets with older brothers fighting in the Confederate army who were VMI graduates. Captain A.P. Hill, tactical commander of Company C of the cadets during the battle, had graduated from VMI in 1859. Henry Wise, who took command of the cadets during the battle after Colonel Shipp was wounded, was a graduate of VMI in 1862. So the real value of VMI during the Civil War was as the training ground for Confederate officers.

However you look at the Corps of Cadets and its role in the Battle of New Market, the fact that they fought together as a unit in a real battle remains an important part of the school's spirit today. Members of the "Rat" class, as first year students are known, today are lectured on their proud history, including the New Market battle, by the Secretary of the Army. They are brought to New Market and there they march in their first parade as cadets and then are shown a re-enactment of the battle. Finally they charge up the final hill that the cadets charged on May 15, 1864. Their chaplain then talks to them about what the battle means to them. The experience stays with them and its powerful effect is very evident when they speak of it.

Cadet John D. Shorter (VMI 1991), who is related to Cadet John W. Wyatt who fought in the battle, comes

This is the Bushong House today. It is part of the battlefield park and is being restored. (Courtesy of Virginia Military Institute.)

from a family where the VMI tradition is part of family history—his grandfather's ashes were spread over the Statue of Virginia Mourning her Dead at VMI. He says of VMI: "There's something special about this school—a spirit that no other school I looked at has . . . we have tradition, we have commitment, we have honor . . . We use as our example that these young boys go out to die at the Battle of New Market; [that] shows the sense of commitment, duty and honor . . . that's something that bonds us."

Cadet Christopher Whittaker (VMI 1990) describes it as "kind of the citizen-soldier concept that Virginia has and the United States has . . . The cadets were looked down upon but they had discipline, they had spirit, they persevered."

Today you can walk the fields where the cadets fought and died at the New Market Battlefield Historical Park. You can see some of the weapons they used and the clothes they wore in the Museums both at the battlefield's Hall of Valor and at VMI in Lexington. You can drive along Route 11 and follow the path they marched from Lexington to New Market. Although the Battle of New Market was not one of the most important battles of the Civil War, the memory of this fight has lasted much longer than other battles its size. For that, all of the credit goes to the Corps of Cadets since they fought well despite their youth and inexperience. It is their involvement that made this battle much more memorable that anyone would have ever expected it to be.

There is one other very special way in which the memory of the battle is kept alive. In May 1866, a detail of cadets was sent to New Market to escort back to Lexington the bodies of five of the cadets killed in the battle. The five, who had been buried at New Market after the battle, were Cadets Atwill, Jefferson, Jones,

Copies of vouchers for the expenses of bringing back to Lexington the bodies of five of the Cadets for burial in the Cadet Cemetery at VMI. (Courtesy of Virginia Military Institute Archives.)

*In May 1866 the bodies of five of the cadets who had
been buried at New Market were returned to VMI
and buried in the Cadet Cemetery there. (Courtesy of
Virginia Military Institute Archives.)*

McDowell, and Wheelwright. The bodies were then buried in the Cadet Cemetery on the grounds of VMI on May 15, 1866, the second anniversary of the battle.

In 1912 a monument called "Virginia Mourning her Dead" by former cadet Moses Ezekiel was dedicated at VMI. Ezekiel had been the roommate of Cadet Thomas Garland Jefferson who had died in the battle. The five cadets were reburied at the monument. Then on May 15, 1960, ninety-six years after the battle, the remains of Cadet Charles Crockett were brought to VMI and reinterred with those of the other five cadets.

This was done on New Market Day because this ceremony has become the most famous of all the ways the battle is remembered. Every year on May 15th, the academy has a special ceremony to honor the cadets who fought as adults in the Battle of New Market. The names of the cadets who fought and died in the battle are called in a special roll call. With the whole Cadet Corps standing at attention, one of today's cadets who has been given the honor, calls out for his cadet's name, "Dead on the field of Honor." Cadet Whittaker says that this is one of the "neatest" ceremonies of the whole year because this one serves a purpose, "Honoring the whole principle of what a soldier stands for, dying for his country." Cadet Shorter notes that there is some "joking around" at most of the parades, "but not at New Market [Day], not a word; it's dead calm . . . it absolutely brings chills down your spine."

Two hundred and sixty-four boys, ages fifteen to nineteen, who fought as adults in a battle. Ten who fought their first and last battle on those fields of New Market, Virginia.

Cadet Moses Ezekiel lived through the battle and went on to become a world famous sculptor. But he never forgot the cadets who died, especially his roommate, Thomas Garland Jefferson. He designed a memorial to the cadets, which is at VMI today. (Courtesy of Virginia Military Institute Archives.)

New Market Day Ceremony at VMI, May 15, 1967. The statue, by Moses Ezekiel, is called Virginia Mourning Her Dead. (Courtesy of Virginia Military Institute Archives.)

SOURCES
FOR RESEARCH

Since there are not many books written about the Battle of New Market, in researching this book I spent most of my time working with primary source material from the Archives in Preston Library at the Virginia Military Institute. They have there a file on every cadet who has ever attended VMI along with collections of all sorts of interesting material for learning the stories of the cadets. The collection of letters from the cadets remembering the details of the battle makes fantastic reading. But there was even more. I held in my hands the last letter Cadet Stanard wrote to his mother, picked out the names of the cadets I knew from the old Matriculation Registers, looked at some of the original drawings done by Moses Ezekiel, and got to see a great deal of interesting artifacts. Working with the archival material is great fun.

Working with archival material can also be very frustrating. One of the things you learn very quickly is that some of the information you need is either wrong or not there. Take, for example, the number of cadets involved in the battle. Because VMI was burned down just two months after the battle, some of the information we need to see to discover how many cadets actually fought in the battle is missing. We have no way of knowing exactly which cadets were there, which ones stayed behind at VMI, and which ones might have been at home at the time. I have tried to pick the "best" numbers possible, but I cannot be sure these are the right ones. That kind of thing happens a lot when you work with primary sources.

Another primary source that made for great reading was John S. Wise's *The End of an Era*, which not only gave a poignant firsthand account of what it was like to be a New Market Cadet, but also captured some of the flavor of Southern life during the Civil War.

I was also fortunate to be able to talk with two cadets about what the New Market experience means to cadets at VMI today. Their insights and comments were very inspiring.

The secondary source material is fairly limited because this was not, as I've said before, one of the bigger battles of the Civil War. The most famous account of the battle is by Edward Raymond Turner, *The New Market Campaign, May 1864*, (Richmond, 1912). William C. Davis's *The Battle of New Market* (New York, 1975) is the newest source. Mr. Davis's book covers the whole battle in all its complexity, although I was most interested in the cadets' role in the battle. There were three VMI books which I found to be very useful. The first of these was William Couper's *The VMI New Market Cadets* (Charlottesville, 1933), a particularly useful source that led me to the files on the cadets in the Archives. Jenning C. Wise's *The Military History of the Virginia Military Institute from 1839 to 1865* (Lynchburg, 1915) and William Couper's *One Hundred Years at VMI* (Richmond, 1959) also provided some very interesting background information. A book entitled *A Virginia Military Institute Album, 1839-1910* by Archivist Diane B. Jacob and Judith Arnold (Charlottesville, 1982) introduced me to the wealth of photographic materials available on VMI. Finally, there were assorted pamphlets published about the battle that were quite helpful, along with several articles in *The Confederate Veteran* and *Civil War Times Illustrated*, which provided good overviews of the battle.

INDEX